W9-BXT-242

# War and Conflict in the Middle East™

# The Gulf War

## Suzanne J. Murdico

The Rosen Publishing Group, Inc., New York

*For my sister and brother-in-law: Darien Eckert Kowell and Jeffry A. Kowell, Master Sergeant, U.S. Army*

Published in 2004 by The Rosen Publishing Group, Inc.
29 East 21st Street, New York, NY 10010

Copyright © 2004 by The Rosen Publishing Group, Inc.

First Edition

All rights reserved. No part of this book may be reproduced in any form without permission in writing from the publisher, except by a reviewer.

**Library of Congress Cataloging-in-Publication Data**

Murdico, Suzanne J.
The Gulf War / by Suzanne J. Murdico.— 1st ed.
    p. cm. — (War and conflict in the Middle East)
Summary: Examines events surrounding the 1991 war between Iraq and a worldwide coalition of forces, plus biographical notes on important figures and a look at the effects of this war.
Includes bibliographical references (p. ) and index.
ISBN 0-8239-4551-0 (library binding)
1. Persian Gulf War, 1991—Juvenile literature. [1. Persian Gulf War, 1991.] I. Title. II. Series.
DS79.723.M87 2003
956.7044'2—dc22

2003016117

*Manufactured in the United States of America*

# CONTENTS

INTRODUCTION                                        4

CHAPTER 1  PRELUDE TO WAR                           8

CHAPTER 2  FORMING A COALITION                     16

CHAPTER 3  AIR STRIKES                             24

CHAPTER 4  GROUND OFFENSIVE                        32

CHAPTER 5  GULF WAR LEGACY                         42

GLOSSARY                                           58

FOR MORE INFORMATION                               60

FOR FURTHER READING                                61

BIBLIOGRAPHY                                       62

INDEX                                              63

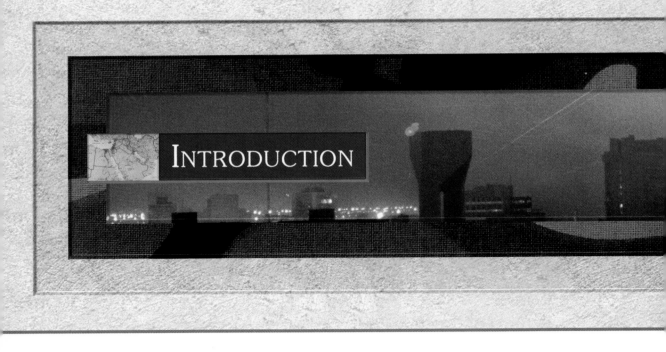

# INTRODUCTION

It began in the early morning hours of January 17, 1991. The predawn sky over Baghdad suddenly brightened with the red and white lights of antiaircraft fire. Baghdad is the capital of Iraq, a large country in the Middle East. Loud explosions and the sounds of antiaircraft weapons could be heard booming throughout the city. The sights and sounds of warfare were coming from fighter jets dropping bombs on strategic targets located in and around Baghdad. Coalition troops from the United States and countries around the world had begun a massive air strike on Iraq.

Almost as soon as the attacks started, live pictures were transmitted around the globe. Reporters from CNN (Cable News Network) provided commentary on what they saw and heard from their hotel rooms in Baghdad. These air strikes were the beginning of the Persian Gulf War, also called the Gulf War. It would become the first war to be shown live on television.

Although the war didn't really begin until the allied air strikes in January 1991, the stage had been set back in August 1990. That was when Iraq's dictator, Saddam Hussein, and his army invaded the tiny neighboring country of Kuwait. Iraq and Kuwait had a history of disputes over land, money, and oil. Although Kuwait is a small country, it has a prime location on the Persian Gulf. Kuwait's vast resources of oil have enabled the country to become very wealthy.

During the 1980s, Iraq had been involved in a long battle with Iran, another neighboring country. At the end of the Iran-Iraq War (1980–1988), there was no clear winner, and Iraq was left with a great deal of debt. Saddam Hussein then set his sights on Iraq's wealthy neighbor to the southeast. On August 2, 1990, the Iraqi army invaded Kuwait.

The Iraqi invasion of Kuwait outraged people around the world. If Iraq could invade Kuwait, what country would be next? How could any country be assured of its safety against Iraq's mighty army? At the start of the Gulf War, Iraq had the second-strongest military in the Middle East. The only Middle Eastern country with a stronger military was Israel. The country of Saudi Arabia, in particular, was concerned about the possibility of an Iraqi attack. Saudi Arabia shares its northern border with both Iraq and Kuwait.

The United Nations (UN) tried diplomatic measures to get Iraq to leave Kuwait. But Saddam Hussein stubbornly refused to withdraw his troops. President George H. W. Bush and his advisers decided that it was time for the United

Two attack squadron 72 A-73 Corsair aircraft fly toward their targets during Operation Desert Storm.

States to become involved in the Iraq-Kuwait conflict. Bush's plan brought together a coalition of troops from countries around the world. It was code-named Operation Desert Shield. The coalition troops were stationed in the Middle East to protect, or shield, Saudi Arabia and other neighboring countries from possible attack by Iraqi forces.

Between August 1990 and January 1991, several attempts were made to get Iraq to peacefully withdraw from Kuwait without a war. These attempts failed. The UN Security Council set a deadline of January 15 for Iraq to withdraw its forces from Kuwait. The deadline passed with Iraq still holding its ground in Kuwait. On January 17, Operation Desert Shield became Operation Desert Storm as allied forces began the most powerful air assault in history.

In the first twenty-four hours of Operation Desert Storm, allied forces flew more than 1,000 air missions—known as sorties—over Iraq. These air and missile attacks targeted Iraqi transportation and communications systems, as well as military installations and ground forces. By the end of the air campaign's first week, fighter planes and fighter-bombers from a number of coalition nations had flown 8,000 sorties. The total number of sorties flown during the course of the Gulf War was a whopping 110,000.

After six weeks of being pummeled by allied air strikes, Iraqi troops were tired, scared, and hungry. Saddam Hussein, however, was still not willing to withdraw his forces from Kuwait. It would take a 100-hour ground assault before the Persian Gulf War would finally come to an end.

# CHAPTER 1

## PRELUDE TO WAR

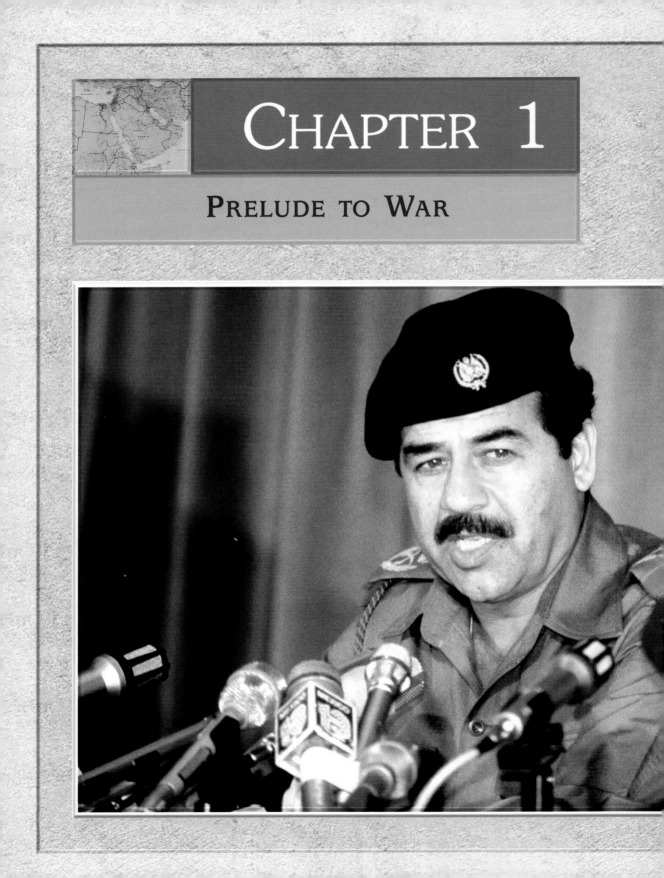

In 1979, a new leader began to shake things up in the Middle East. Saddam Hussein, a man with a great desire for wealth, land, and power became the new ruler of Iraq. Hussein had already established a reputation as a ruthless military leader. On September 22, 1980—just one year after taking over as president of Iraq—Hussein and his army invaded the neighboring country of Iran. Ten years later, they would invade Kuwait, setting off the Persian Gulf War.

## Iran-Iraq War

Iraq and Iran have a long history of disputes over territory and politics. Iraq's invasion of Iran in 1980 started a war that would last for much of the decade. With the invasion, Saddam Hussein wanted to gain control of the Shatt al Arab waterway. This waterway, located on the border between Iran and Iraq, leads to the Persian Gulf. Controlling the waterway would give Iraq more control over the region's oil resources and enable Saddam Hussein to extend Iraq's boundaries.

The Iran-Iraq War dragged on for many years with neither side gaining any territory. The war was costly in terms of both money and lives lost. In 1988, the Iran-Iraq War finally ended when the United Nations negotiated a cease-fire between

Taken in November 1980, this photo of Iraqi President Saddam Hussein shows the dictator looking more exuberant and youthful than in 1991 and again in 2003, when Baghdad was bombed.

Francoise de Mulder took this photo of Iraqi soldiers in a tank in 1980 during the Iran-Iraq War. The men were stationed at the Khorramshahr front and ready for battle.

the two countries. But the long war had left Iraq's economy in serious trouble.

## Iraq's Disputes with Kuwait

Before the invasion of Kuwait, Iraq had three main complaints with its tiny neighbor Kuwait. Some of these complaints had their origins in recent events, while others had been going on for many years. One dispute involved money that Iraq had borrowed from Kuwait during the Iran-Iraq War. A second dispute was over the amount of oil being produced by Kuwait. The third dispute involved the border between Iraq and Kuwait and the vast oil field that lies beneath it.

### Iraq's Debt to Kuwait

During the 1980s, Iraq had borrowed money from several of its Middle Eastern neighbors. The money was used to help pay for the Iran-Iraq War. By the end of the war, Iraq owed Kuwait billions of dollars. When it came time to begin repaying the debt, Saddam Hussein balked. He felt that Iraq should not have to pay back Kuwait. He reasoned that Iraq had been protecting Kuwait from Iran and its Muslim fundamentalist leader, Ayatollah Khomeini. According to Hussein, Iraq's debt to Kuwait should have been canceled as payment for this protection.

### Kuwait's Oil Production

Another source of Saddam Hussein's anger with Kuwait stemmed from Kuwait's production of oil. Hussein accused Kuwait and the United Arab Emirates of producing more oil than allowed by the Organization of Petroleum Exporting

This is a photograph of an oil refinery in Kuwait. When coalition troops forced Iraqi soldiers to leave Kuwait, they destroyed refineries and burned oil in the fields as an act of revenge so no one could use the oil.

Countries (OPEC). This overproduction, Hussein argued, increased world oil supplies, thus lowering oil prices. Lower oil prices meant that Iraq made less profit on the sale of its oil. By Saddam Hussein's estimates, these lower prices resulted in Iraq's loss of $14 billion in oil revenues.

## Iraq-Kuwait Border

The dispute over the border between Iraq and Kuwait dates back 100 years or more. In the late 1800s and early 1900s, Kuwait was part of Basra, a province of the Ottoman Empire. Years later, Basra became part of Iraq. By that time, Kuwait was no longer part of Basra and therefore did not become part of Iraq. In the 1920s, both Kuwait and Iraq came under British rule. Both countries eventually gained their independence—Iraq in 1932 and Kuwait in 1961. After becoming an independent nation, Kuwait continued to have border disputes with Iraq. Although Kuwait is a much smaller country than Iraq, Kuwait's coastline is much longer than Iraq's. Kuwait's location allows convenient access to the Persian Gulf and an important harbor that allows easier shipping of its oil to the world market. Iraq has no large harbor on the gulf. It does have an important port along the Shatt al Arab River. But Iraq shares the river with Iran. Iraq wanted more and easier access to oil and shipping methods.

　　Another source of the Iraq-Kuwait border debate involved the Rumaila oil field. Straddling the Iraq-Kuwait border, the Rumaila oil field is Iraq's largest and most important oil field.

## GULF WAR BIO
## Saddam Hussein

Saddam Hussein was president of Iraq from 1979 until 2003, when he was removed from power during the second Gulf War. Hussein was born in 1937 in Tikrit in northern Iraq, and his parents were peasants. He joined the Baath Party in 1957 and, two years later, took part in an attempt to assassinate the Iraqi prime minister Abdul Karim Kassem. Following that unsuccessful attempt, Hussein fled to Syria and later Egypt. He attended law school in Cairo and then in Baghdad

Saddam Hussein at a Baghdad military parade in 2000.

after returning to Iraq in 1963. That year, the Baathists had taken power, but they were soon overthrown by a military coup. Hussein spent several years in prison before eventually escaping in 1966.

Hussein became a leader of the Baath Party and played an important role in the 1968 coup that returned the party to power. During the early 1970s, he oversaw the nationalization of the oil industry in Iraq. In 1979, Iraq's president resigned, and Hussein took over that position. Although he remained in power after the first Gulf War, coalition forces brought down Hussein's government during the second Gulf War. In mid-2003, it was not known whether Saddam Hussein was alive or dead.

Before the invasion, Iraq accused Kuwait of stealing oil from this field. The claim was that Kuwait used slant drilling to drill under Iraq to take oil from the Rumaila field.

## Invasion of Kuwait

During the summer of 1990, Iraq made several unsuccessful attempts to resolve its disputes with Kuwait. When the disputes were not resolved, Saddam Hussein issued warnings that he would take military action against Kuwait. His threats were not taken seriously until August 2, 1990. In the early morning hours of that day, 100,000 Iraqi soldiers and hundreds of tanks crossed over Iraq's border with Kuwait.

To the great surprise of the world, Iraq quickly seized Kuwait and its vast oil resources. Kuwait's small army was no match for Iraq's army, which was the fifth largest in the world. Complete Iraqi control over Kuwait was achieved in just twenty-four hours. Soon after, Iraq began moving thousands of troops to Kuwait's border with Saudi Arabia. It looked as though Iraq was planning to invade Saudi Arabia as well.

On August 8, 1990, Saddam Hussein declared that Kuwait had been annexed to Iraq. Despite Iraq's disputes with Kuwait, an invasion was not warranted under international law. Although a few Arab countries supported the Iraqi invasion, the United States and most other countries around the world criticized it. The United Nations also condemned Iraq's move. It would soon become clear that military action would be needed to force Iraq to withdraw its troops from Kuwait and to prevent an invasion of Saudi Arabia.

# CHAPTER 2

## FORMING A COALITION

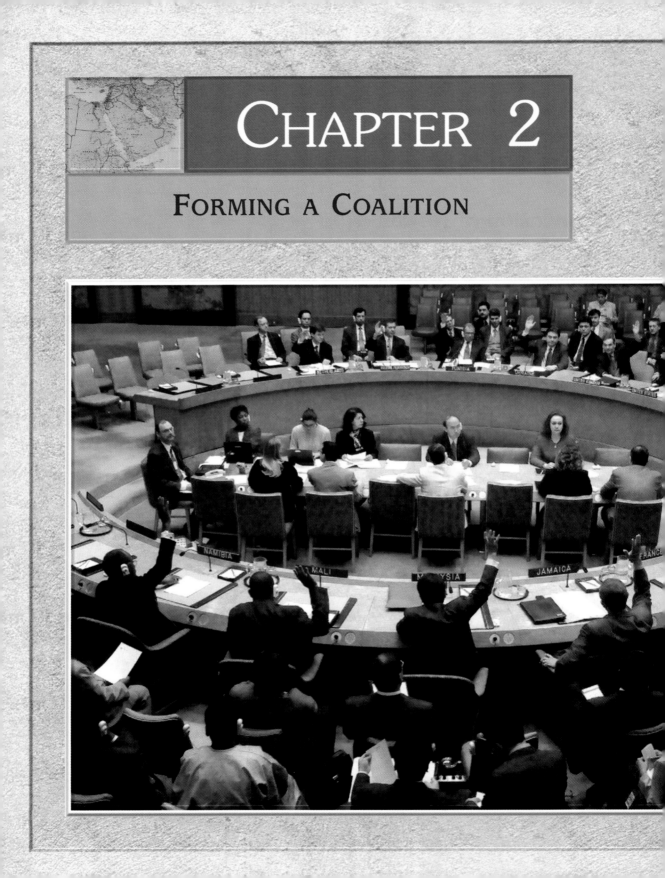

At the time of the Gulf War, Iraq and Kuwait's combined oil reserves totaled nearly 200 billion barrels. Saudi Arabia's oil reserves were estimated at more than 250 billion barrels. The oil reserves of these three countries made up 45 percent of the total oil reserves in the world. It's easy to see, then, why Saddam Hussein seized Kuwait's oil wells and also wanted to take control over Saudi Arabia's wells. It's also easy to understand why so many countries around the world, including the United States, took a serious interest in the events unfolding in the Middle East.

## UN Sanctions

On August 2, 1990—the same day that Iraq invaded Kuwait—the United Nations issued a resolution condemning the invasion. The resolution called for Iraq's immediate withdrawal from Kuwait. Four days later, the UN Security Council imposed economic sanctions on Iraq. A trade embargo banned all countries from trade with Iraq. The only exceptions were items of humanitarian aid, such as food and medical supplies.

The trade embargo meant that Iraq would not be able to sell the oil that it produced, making it very difficult for the country to earn money. In addition, the embargo prevented Iraq from importing goods that

On August 6, 1990 members of the United Nations Security Council voted to impose a trade embargo on Iraq for its invasion of Kuwait four days earlier.

the country needed. The goal of the embargo was to force Iraq into complying with the UN resolution by creating major economic hardship for the country.

## Atrocities in Kuwait

Not long after Iraq invaded Kuwait, news began to spread about atrocities occurring in Kuwait. Before the invasion, about 9,000 people from North America, Europe, and Australia were living and working in Kuwait and Iraq. In the middle of August, Saddam Hussein declared that these civilians were now hostages. Many of these hostages were taken to military bases and other strategic locations in Iraq and Kuwait. The hostages would serve as "human shields" against attack by allied forces. Saddam Hussein thought that the allies would not risk hurting their own people in an attack. By early December, Hussein had let all the hostages leave the region.

Worse yet, there were also many stories of crimes and brutality against Kuwaiti civilians after the occupation by Iraq. A great deal of physical damage was done to the country, and Iraqi soldiers looted homes, stores, and public buildings. There were also stories of torture, rape, and murder of Kuwaitis. People suspected of being resistance fighters were executed. These atrocities made it all the more crucial that Iraq be forced to leave Kuwait.

## Preparing for War

Just after Iraq's invasion of Kuwait, the U.S. government convinced King Faud, the ruler of Saudi Arabia, to allow

## GULF WAR BIO
## George H. W. Bush

George H. W. Bush spent many years in the White House. From 1981 to 1989, he served as vice president of the United States under President Ronald Reagan. Bush then went on to serve one term as the forty-first president of the United States (1989–1993). One of five children, George Herbert Walker Bush was born in 1924 in Milton, Massachusetts. His father was an investment banker who later became a U.S. senator from Connecticut. George H. W. Bush served as a torpedo bomber pilot during World War II and received the Distinguished Flying Cross for heroism.

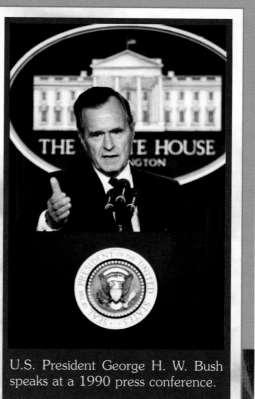

U.S. President George H. W. Bush speaks at a 1990 press conference.

In 1945, Bush married Barbara Pierce. After the war, he attended Yale University and graduated in 1948 with a bachelor's degree in economics. He turned down a position with his father's investment banking firm. Instead, he decided to move to Texas to pursue a career in oil. Beginning in 1959, Bush became active in politics. Before becoming vice president, he held various political positions, including representative in the U.S. House of Representatives, U.S. ambassador to the United Nations, and chairman of the Republican National Committee. George and Barbara Bush had six children. One son—George W. Bush—was elected governor of Texas and then president of the United States in 2000. Another son—Jeb Bush—was elected governor of Florida.

American troops to enter the country. The United States wanted to help Saudi Arabia defend itself against a possible invasion by Iraq. Within two weeks, 30,000 U.S. troops were stationed in Saudi Arabia.

## Gathering Forces

President George H. W. Bush began contacting other world leaders to form a coalition against Iraq. More and more countries joined the coalition until it eventually included thirty-nine

On January 22, 1991, French and American troops travel together along the Iraqi border during the Gulf War. Saddam Hussein's invasion of Kuwait provoked a coalition of countries to try and expel his forces.

nations. President Bush called the coalition the New World Order. The buildup of troops and equipment in the Persian Gulf region became known as Operation Desert Shield.

By the middle of January, coalition troops stationed in the Persian Gulf numbered 670,000, including 425,000 U.S. troops. A large portion of the remaining troops came from Great Britain and France, along with the Arab nations of Saudi Arabia, Egypt, and Syria. Not all coalition members sent troops to the Persian Gulf. Some provided equipment, supplies, or monetary aid. In addition to troops, coalition resources in the Persian Gulf included 3,500 tanks, 1,800 combat aircraft, and 200 warships.

## Two Generals

Having large numbers of troops and equipment ready for action was an essential part of the plan during Operation Desert Shield. But the troops are only as good as their leaders. President Bush's top two military advisers—General Colin Powell and General H. Norman Schwarzkopf—were essential in planning and carrying out the operation. As chairman of the Joint Chiefs of Staff, General Powell was President Bush's top military adviser. He was in charge of handling communication between the battlefield and the White House. As commander of the coalition forces, General Schwarzkopf planned the military actions that took place during the war.

## The Mother of All Battles

While coalition forces prepared to take military action against Iraq, Iraqi forces prepared to stand their ground in

## Women in the Gulf War

Nearly 40,000 American women served in the 1991 Gulf War. It was the largest deployment of women in U.S. military history. At the time, a federal law prohibited women from taking part in combat. Instead, the women of the Gulf War worked in supporting roles. Some served as pilots on noncombat missions, such as transporting supplies, ammunition, and soldiers. Other women drove trucks, worked as mechanics, or served as military police officers. During the Gulf War, fifteen women died serving their country.

A female American soldier in Dhahran, Saudi Arabia, is prepared to support combat troops in a noncombat role.

Following the Gulf War, a bill was introduced in Congress that repealed the law barring women from flying combat missions. After the bill became a law, the U.S. military began training women in combat aircraft.

Kuwait. Iraq's military leaders told Iraqi citizens to get ready for "the mother of all battles." By October 1990, Iraq had 300,000 troops positioned on the gulf coast of Kuwait and also on the border between Kuwait and Saudi Arabia. Many of the Iraqi soldiers in the front lines were civilians who were recruited for the Gulf War. They were reported to be poorly trained and poorly supplied.

## The UN Deadline

On November 29, 1990, the UN Security Council set a deadline of January 15, 1991, for Iraq to withdraw from Kuwait. If Iraq chose not to leave, the council authorized the coalition members to use "all means necessary" to expel Iraqi forces from Kuwait. The allies were ready to launch air and ground attacks, but they waited to see how Iraq would respond to the UN deadline.

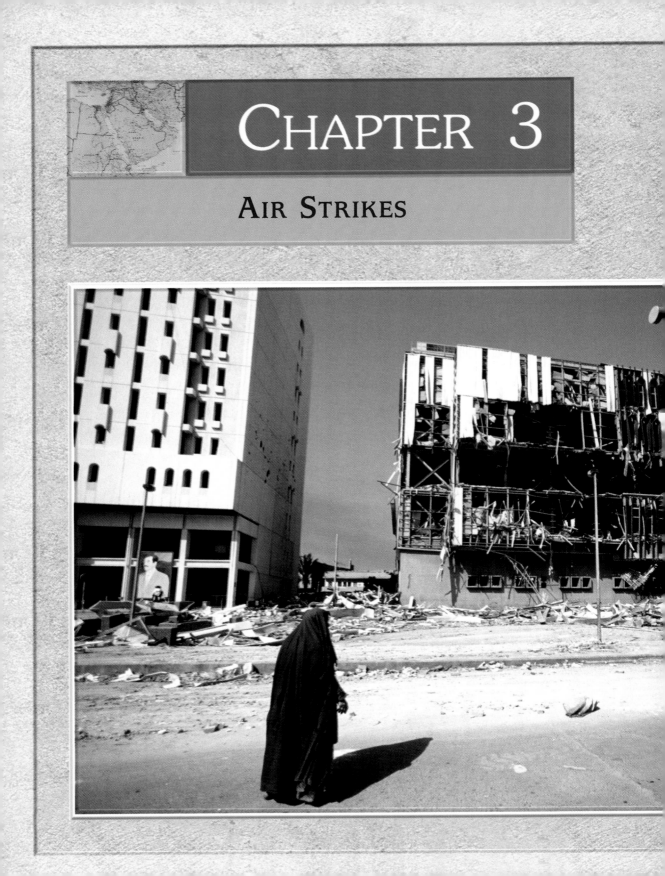

# CHAPTER 3

## AIR STRIKES

On January 15, 1991, the last hope vanished for a peaceful resolution to Iraq's occupation of Kuwait. That date was the UN Security Council's deadline for Iraq to withdraw its troops. When Iraq did not comply, coalition forces prepared to launch Operation Desert Storm.

## The Storm Begins

At 4 AM on January 17, the first allied air strikes began in the skies over Iraq. The first bombs landed on the country's capital

of Baghdad. The allies then bombed targets elsewhere in Iraq and also in Kuwait. The main objective of the air war was to destroy Iraq's equipment and supplies. One of the first specific goals was to make it impossible for Iraq to launch attacks against the allies.

Many targets of the allied forces were military. They bombed military command posts, airfields and aircraft bunkers, and ammunition warehouses. Other targets included Iraqi transportation networks, such as roads and bridges, and communication systems. Allied air strikes also targeted the supply lines that provided Iraqi troops with food, water, and ammunition. Another goal of the air war was to reduce the number of Iraqi

In this photo, a lone woman observes the massive destruction of a bombed communications center in Baghdad, Iraq, on February 27, 1991.

## High-Tech Weapons

During the Persian Gulf War, U.S. troops were very successful in their fight against Iraqi forces. A number of high-tech—and high-cost—weapons helped the U.S. troops achieve this success.

- **F-117A Stealth Fighters**—With a price tag of more than $100 million each, F-117A stealth fighters were very expensive—and secret—weapons of war. These planes were uniquely designed to avoid detection by enemy radar. The stealth fighters have an unusual arrowhead shape and a special covering that absorbs and deflects radio waves. This design makes the stealth invisible on enemy radar screens.
- **Tomahawk Cruise Missiles**—Costing more than $1 million each, Tomahawk cruise missiles were another type of high-tech weapon. These missiles were able to stay out of range of enemy radar because they flew at extremely low altitudes. On the first day of Operation Desert Storm, 100 Tomahawk missiles were fired at enemy targets.
- **Smart Bombs**—About 7 percent of all bombs dropped during the Gulf War were "smart bombs." These bombs, weighing 2,000 pounds (907 kilograms) each, are equipped with lasers that guide them to their target. The accuracy of smart bombs in hitting their intended military targets helped reduce the number of civilian casualties.
- **Patriot Missiles**—A surface-to-air missile (used to strike aircraft from the ground), the Patriot weighs 2,200 pounds (998 kg) and has a range of about 43 miles (69 kilometers). During the Gulf War, Patriots were launched at incoming Iraqi Scud missiles in an attempt to destroy them before they reached the ground.
- **Apache Helicopters**—An attack helicopter, the Apache was specifically designed for attacking enemy targets on the ground. Apaches are armed with antitank missiles that can penetrate the armor of enemy tanks and other vehicles. The Apache's own armor protects the helicopter's crew and vital systems from attack.

troops. Of special interest were Iraq's elite Republican Guard units. Members of the Republican Guard were considered to be the best fighters in Iraq's army.

## Iraq's Response

Less than twenty-four hours after the coalition's air strikes began, Iraq retaliated by launching Scud missiles at Israel and Saudi Arabia. Scud missiles were surface-to-surface missiles that had been manufactured by the Soviet Union. They were designed to launch from the ground to hit targets also on the ground. Compared with the high-tech weapons used by the allies, Scud missiles were outdated and crude. They were not guided by lasers, and they had a poor level of accuracy in hitting targets.

In some ways, the inaccuracy of the Scud missiles made the attacks all the more frightening. The missiles were more likely to hit unintended targets, such as homes, schools, and civilians. In addition, it was feared that Saddam Hussein might arm the Scud missiles with chemical warheads. Hussein had used chemical weapons in the past against his own people. As it turns out, he did not use them during the Gulf War.

### Attack on Israel

Even though the Israelis were not taking part in the war with Iraq, the main target of Iraq's Scud missiles was Israel. Scuds were launched on two major Israeli cities—Tel Aviv and Haifa. With these attacks, Saddam Hussein hoped to

A man holding a gas mask surveys a damaged building in southern Tel Aviv on January 18, 1991. The building was cut in half by an Iraqi Scud missile.

bully Israel into fighting back and thereby entering the war. Israel is an ally of the United States. But it's a longtime enemy of Arab nations, including Saudi Arabia, Egypt, and Syria. If Israel fought back, the Arab nations might have viewed the war as an Arab-Israeli conflict. In that event, the Arab nations would most likely leave the coalition. This action would severely weaken the power of the coalition forces against Saddam Hussein and his army.

It was vital, then, that Israel did not retaliate against Iraq and enter the Gulf War. Although the Israelis wanted to fight back, President Bush convinced them to stay out of the war. The United States immediately sent Patriot missile launchers to Israel to intercept Iraq's incoming Scud missiles. U.S. military forces also vowed that future air strikes would focus on destroying Iraqi Scud installations. These actions kept Israel from entering the war, and the coalition stayed intact.

## Iraqi Defense

Besides the Scud missile attacks, Iraqi forces did very little in the way of responding to the allied air war. Instead of a true plan of defense, the Iraqi strategy seemed to be to simply stay out of the way of the air strikes. Although Iraq had air forces, they never got very involved in fighting against the allies. Unlike the coalition air forces, the Iraqi air forces played a very small role in the Gulf War.

During the first days of the allied air strikes, Iraq's planes never even left the ground. As the air war continued,

## GULF WAR BIO
### Colin Powell

General Colin Powell is a man of many "firsts." In 1989, he became the first African American to serve as chairman of the Joint Chiefs of Staff. He was appointed secretary of state of the United States in 2001, becoming the first African American to hold that position. Born in 1937, Colin L. Powell grew up in New York City. His parents were immigrants from Jamaica. Powell graduated from the City College of New York in 1958 and was commissioned a second lieutenant in the U.S. Army.

In September 1990, General Colin Powell toured military facilities in Saudi Arabia.

During the Vietnam War, Powell served two tours of duty. After the war, he earned a master's degree from George Washington University in Washington, D.C. For several years, he commanded troops both in the United States and abroad, and he held various posts, including some at the Pentagon. In 1987, President Ronald Reagan appointed Powell to the position of assistant to the president for national security affairs. Powell became a four-star general in 1989 and also took over the Army Forces Command. Later that year, President George H. W. Bush appointed him chairman of the Joint Chiefs of Staff. Powell retired from the U.S. Army in 1993.

some Iraqi planes took to the skies. Allied forces shot down several of them. Then, oddly, Iraqi pilots began moving planes to Iran. During the Gulf War, Iran was not on the side of Iraq nor was it on the side of the coalition. Iran had declared that it was a neutral country. It was speculated that Iraq moved the planes to Iran so they wouldn't be destroyed in the war.

# CHAPTER 4

## GROUND OFFENSIVE

The goal of the massive air strikes was to destroy the Iraqi army while incurring as few allied casualties as possible. The heavy bombing was an attempt to force Iraq to withdraw from Kuwait. After more than five weeks, however, Iraq still would not leave Kuwait. With Iraqi forces severely weakened, coalition forces were then able to enter Kuwait and Iraq on the ground. They encountered little resistance. In just 100 hours, ground forces would retake Kuwait City and liberate the Kuwaiti people.

## Final Attempt at Peace

Before the ground war began, one final attempt at a peace agreement was made. All along, the Soviet Union and its leader, Mikhail Gorbachev, had been in favor of getting Iraq to leave Kuwait without resorting to war. Although the Soviet Union did support the coalition forces, Gorbachev questioned the need to destroy Iraq. He was also concerned that Iraqi civilians were being needlessly killed.

Gorbachev began working on a peace agreement that could put an end to the war before the ground assault began. After meetings between Soviet and Iraqi diplomats, a possible agreement was announced. The agreement was not without conditions, however. Iraq would withdraw its forces

A group of American Special Forces watches the horizon, weapons ready, looking for movement from the Iraqis. Saudi and Kuwaiti troops also helped the coalition against Saddam Hussein.

American troops take an Iraqi soldier prisoner as coalition forces move toward Kuwait City in February 1991.

from Kuwait if Israel could be compelled to withdraw from Palestinian territories. Arab nations felt that these territories did not rightfully belong to Israel. As a second condition of the agreement, Iraq would not have to pay for any damage sustained by Kuwait during the Iraqi invasion. Because of these two conditions, President Bush and the U.S. government did not accept the peace agreement.

President Bush then issued an ultimatum to Saddam Hussein. Iraq must accept all UN resolutions and begin withdrawing troops by noon on February 23, 1991, or risk an all-out ground assault. The deadline passed with Iraqi troops still occupying Kuwait.

## Operation Desert Sabre

Allied forces were prepared for the ground assault on Iraqi troops—code-named Operation Desert Sabre. General H. Norman Schwarzkopf, commander of the allied forces, had devised a clever plan of attack. The first part of the plan involved tricking Saddam Hussein. The second part of the plan involved a three-pronged ground offensive by the allied forces. The ultimate goal was to reclaim Kuwait from the Iraqis.

### Surprising Saddam

Before the ground war began, coalition forces stationed many navy ships in the Persian Gulf, near the Kuwaiti coast. Thousands of U.S. Marines onboard these ships took part in a variety of amphibious maneuvers. Although it

## GULF WAR BIO
## H. Norman Schwarzkopf

General "Stormin' Norman" Schwarzkopf is probably best known for his leadership role during the Persian Gulf War. However, he is also a highly decorated veteran of the Vietnam War of the 1960s and early 1970s. The son of a brigadier general in the U.S. Army, H. Norman Schwarzkopf was born in 1934 in Trenton, New Jersey. In 1956, he graduated from the United States Military Academy and also was commissioned as a second lieutenant in the U.S. Army. In 1964, he graduated from the University of Southern California with a master's degree in mechanical engineering.

General Norman Schwarzkopf, the Commander-in-Chief of Central Command

During the Vietnam War, Schwarzkopf served two tours of duty in Vietnam. After returning to the United States, he commanded troops and worked at the Pentagon. In 1983, he received a promotion to major general and led the ground forces during the U.S. military operation in Grenada. Schwarzkopf was promoted to four-star general in 1988, the same year he was appointed commander in chief of U.S. Central Command. In that position, he was responsible for commanding military operations in the Middle East. In August 1991—shortly after the end of the Gulf War—Schwarzkopf retired from military service.

looked like these actions were being taken to prepare for the ground war, this was not the case. They were performed for the sole purpose of tricking Saddam Hussein into thinking that the allies were planning to attack from Kuwait's gulf coast.

Hussein and his forces fell for the ruse. Iraqi troops positioned themselves along the coast of Kuwait in an effort to stop an attack they thought would come from the Persian Gulf. What the Iraqis didn't know was that General Schwarzkopf had a completely different attack plan in mind. For several weeks, he had been moving thousands of troops, along with tanks, equipment, and supplies, to the west. The Iraqis were unaware of this movement because their air force had been grounded.

## Three-Pronged Attack

During the early morning hours of February 24, 1991, coalition forces began a major ground offensive against the Iraqi army. The attack involved three separate movements of allied ground forces that took place at the same time. In the first movement, American and British troops advanced north from Saudi Arabia into Iraq. The allied troops then headed east to attack Iraqi forces in southern Iraq and northern Kuwait. The Iraqi troops under attack included Saddam Hussein's elite Republican Guard.

The second ground movement included coalition troops from the United States, Saudi Arabia, Kuwait, Egypt, and Syria. These troops moved north from Saudi

This is a photo of the infamous "Highway of Death" in northern Kuwait. As Iraqi military personnel and their families tried to flee Kuwait, coalition forces attacked them. The end result was miles of destruction along this major road.

Arabia, attacking Iraqi forces in southern Kuwait. In the third movement, American and French troops entered Iraq from Saudi Arabia. Veering to the west of Iraqi forces in Kuwait, the coalition troops quickly moved into Iraq. They headed north toward the Euphrates River to cut off Iraqi supply lines and to keep Iraqi troops from escaping into northern Iraq.

## Iraqi Surrender

In two days, allied forces had surrounded the Iraqi troops. With no way out, tens of thousands of Iraqi soldiers quickly surrendered. In addition to dealing with weeks of relentless air attacks, the Iraqi troops were hungry and tired. In many cases, they had been deserted by their commanding officers. Many Iraqi soldiers surrendered happily, knowing they would be given food and allowed to rest. With the surrender of the Iraqi forces, coalition troops were able to reclaim Kuwait's capital city. Kuwaiti citizens, finally liberated from the Iraqi invaders, rejoiced at the arrival of allied troops.

## Cease-Fire

At 8 AM on February 28, 1991—just 100 hours after the ground war had begun—President Bush declared a cease-fire. Coalition forces put an end to all military operations in the region. After Iraq agreed to the terms of a formal cease-fire, the UN Security Council officially declared that the war had ended. According to the terms of the cease-fire

## Gulf War Timeline

### 1990

**August 2** Saddam Hussein and his Iraqi army invade the neighboring country of Kuwait.

**August 2** At an emergency meeting, the UN Security Council demands that Iraqi troops withdraw from Kuwait.

**August 6** The UN Security Council imposes economic sanctions against Iraq.

**August 8** First wave of U.S. troops arrives in Saudi Arabia to help protect the country from a potential Iraqi invasion.

**November 29** The UN Security Council sets a January 15, 1991, deadline for Iraq to withdraw its troops from Kuwait. If the deadline is missed, the council authorizes the use of "all means necessary" to remove Iraqi forces.

### 1991

**January 9** Secretary of State James Baker meets with Iraq's foreign minister, Tariq Aziz, in an attempt to reach a peaceful resolution. The meeting is unsuccessful.

**January 15** The UN deadline for Iraqi troops to leave Kuwait passes. The deadline passes without the Iraqi troops leaving.

**January 17** Allies begin air strikes on Iraqi military and industrial targets.

**February 21** President Bush sets a deadline of February 23 for Iraq to withdraw its forces from Kuwait.

**February 24** Ground war against Iraq begins, lasting for 100 hours.

**February 27** Coalition forces liberate Kuwait City, the capital of Kuwait.

**February 28** Allied attacks against Iraq come to an end as the cease-fire agreement takes effect.

agreement, Iraq was required to destroy all chemical and biological weapons, as well as the factories for manufacturing these weapons. Iraq also agreed to pay Kuwait for damages incurred by the war.

Despite signing the cease-fire agreement, Iraq did not comply with the terms of the contract. As a result, the United Nations continued economic sanctions in an effort to force Iraq into complying. The United Nations–imposed trade embargo on Iraq was not lifted until 2003, when Saddam Hussein was finally removed from power.

# CHAPTER 5

## GULF WAR LEGACY

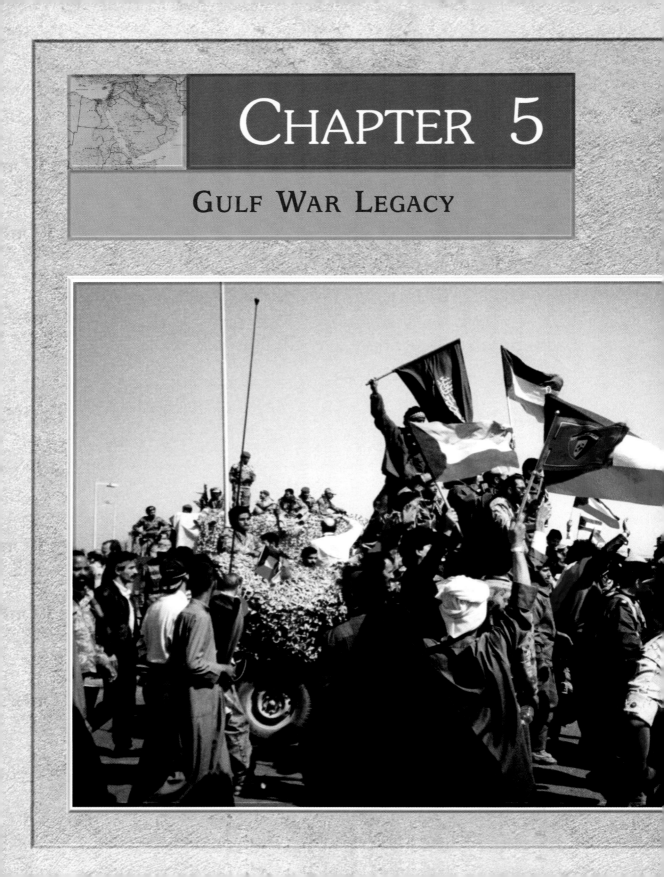

The Gulf War had both positive and negative outcomes. For the United States and its allies, the main objectives of the war were accomplished. The Iraqi forces were driven out of Kuwait, and the country's citizens were liberated. The Kuwaiti government, which was friendly toward the United States, once again controlled Kuwait's rich oil resources. In addition, the numbers of Saddam Hussein's military forces had been severely reduced, and much of their weapons and equipment had been destroyed. Iraq no longer posed a major threat to its neighboring countries, since it would be many years before Iraq could rebuild its military.

On the negative side, many lives were lost during the Gulf War, including about 370 coalition troop members. The allied forces were not able to topple Iraq's government, and Saddam Hussein remained in power after the war. In addition, the war caused a great deal of destruction in both Kuwait and Iraq, where a major cleanup and rebuilding effort was needed. Although the war took place far from the United States, it had negative consequences for Americans.

## Postwar Kuwait

At the end of the Gulf War, Iraqi forces left Kuwait, and the Kuwaiti citizens were free

Civilians and military forces celebrated the Iraqi retreat from Kuwait on February 28, 1991, by waving Kuwaiti, Saudi Arabian, and other flags high above their heads. Operation Desert Storm was over.

once again. But the country was not the same after the war. An estimated 7,000 Kuwaitis died during the Iraqi occupation. Just before the Iraqis withdrew from Kuwait, they had done a great deal of looting. They stole anything of value, including money, vehicles, computer equipment, and furniture. Priceless art and artifacts were stolen from Kuwait's museums. The retreating Iraqis also did what they could to destroy everything else, including Kuwait's oil wells.

## Oil Well Destruction

For Kuwait, one of the most destructive and long-lasting consequences of the Gulf War was the Iraqi attack on its oil wells. Hundreds of oil wells were set on fire, and millions of gallons of oil were spilled on purpose. These oil well attacks were devastating for two main reasons. For one, Kuwait's economy is based largely on income from the sale of oil. So this significant loss of oil affected the country's economy. Even more troublesome, though, was the pollution created by these attacks.

During the war, Iraqi troops had rigged explosives to many of Kuwait's oil wells. As the defeated Iraqis left Kuwait at the end of the war, they set off these explosives. Enormous clouds of acrid black smoke rose from hundreds of burning oil wells. The air pollution created by this smoke could be felt not only in Kuwait but hundreds of miles away. Water was also polluted. During the war, Iraqi forces had dumped nearly 500 million gallons (almost 2 million kiloliters) of oil into the Persian Gulf. It was the

Two C-130 cargo planes fly over burning oil fields near Kuwait City in 1991. After the war, industry experts estimated at the time that the oil field fires were burning 5 to 6 million barrels of crude oil per day.

biggest oil spill in history. The oil slick caused great harm to the environment, killing fish and other wildlife in the gulf and polluting the water and shoreline for many miles.

## The Rebuilding Process

The work of rebuilding Kuwait would be a great challenge. The first hurdle to overcome was the task of putting out the oil well fires that burned out of control. Each of these fires wasted

Oil-well firefighters from around the globe worked around the clock to put out the burning oil wells of Kuwait. The fires were actually put out much more quickly than originally predicted.

precious crude oil and added to the terrible air pollution engulfing the country. To extinguish the oil well fires, Kuwait enlisted the help of experts from the United States. The original estimate for putting out all of the fires was March 1992, but the last major fire was extinguished by November 1991.

With the fires under control, Kuwait could once again start producing oil. However, the country still needed help to restore water and electric power. American engineers were sent to Kuwait to do the job. Slowly, then, the government and people of Kuwait began the long and difficult process of rebuilding their country and economy.

## Postwar Iraq

The people of Kuwait were not the only ones who suffered during the Gulf War. The Iraqi people also had great losses. Allied bombings had devastated the country, destroying buildings, bridges, and roads. The bombs had also taken out electrical power plants and telecommunications systems. The Iraqi people were left with no electricity and very little clean water. Estimates of Iraqi deaths have varied in the years following the war, from 10,000 to over 100,000. Experts today believe Iraqi battlefield deaths were approximately 10,000 to 20,000 Iraqi soldiers and 1,000 to 2,000 civilians.

After the Gulf War, the United Nations continued to impose a trade embargo and other economic sanctions on Iraq. These sanctions banned foreign trade, making it impossible for Iraq to sell its oil abroad. The goal of the UN sanctions was to force Saddam Hussein to comply with the cease-fire agreement, but he refused. The sanctions severely crippled Iraq's economy.

## Disease and Starvation

Bombs and gunshot wounds during the war were not the only things that killed the Iraqis. After the war, disease and starvation plagued the country. The lack of electricity meant that water purification plants stopped working,

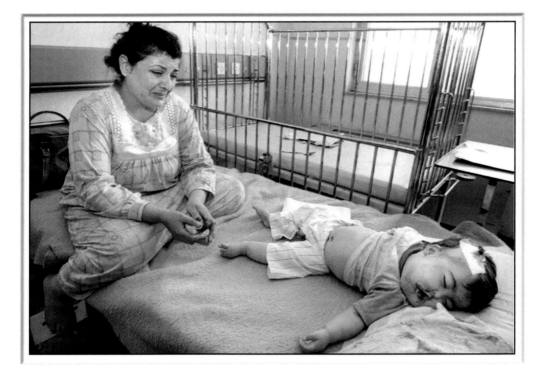

An Iraqi woman grieves by the bedside of her leukemia-stricken child in a Baghdad hospital. His condition may be due to exposure to radioactivity found in the uranium-based weapons used by allied forces in the Gulf War.

leaving the Iraqi people without adequate drinking water. Garbage piled up, and raw sewage ran through the streets. These unsanitary conditions led to outbreaks of cholera, typhoid, and other serious diseases. Medicine and medical treatment were difficult to come by in the months following the war, and many Iraqis died of these illnesses.

The UN sanctions on trade caused food prices to rise dramatically in Iraq. These high prices made it difficult for many Iraqis to buy food. Less than one month after the Gulf War ended, the United Nations lifted the embargo on humanitarian aid and began providing food shipments to Iraq. Even so, other UN sanctions still in effect meant that Iraq could not afford to import enough food for its people. Many Iraqis went hungry, and some died of starvation.

## Civil War

Saddam Hussein remained in power following the Gulf War, but many Iraqis were very unhappy with his leadership. The Kurds, a group of people in northern Iraq, had been opposed to Hussein's rule for many years. In southern Iraq, followers of Islam known as Shiite Muslims also opposed Hussein. Both groups started rebellions against the government, but the Iraqi army quickly suppressed them. Thousands of Kurds and Shiite Muslims were killed during the rebellions.

More than 1 million Kurds became refugees, fleeing to the mountains in northern Iraq. Some continued on to Iran and Turkey. Hundreds of thousands of Shiite

Muslims fled from Iraq to Iran. Some chose to hide in marshy areas of southern Iraq. To protect the Kurdish refugees from the Iraqi army, coalition forces set up a safety zone in northern Iraq. Even after coalition forces left the area, they continued to fly aircraft over northern Iraq to help keep Iraqi forces away. Coalition forces also tried to protect the Shiite refugees by imposing a ban on Iraqi aircraft flights over southern Iraq. Despite these

This image depicts the conditions in a Kurd refugee camp in 1991. When American forces began to withdraw from Iraq, the Kurds feared severe retaliation from the Iraqi army. While the Gulf War was fought, coalition troops protected the Kurds from the Iraqis.

efforts, many Kurdish and Shiite refugees died of starvation, illness, or exposure to the elements.

# U.S. Aftermath of War

Although it didn't take place on U.S. soil, the Persian Gulf War did have a lasting effect on Americans. Financially, the war was expensive and hurt the U.S. economy. The Gulf War took its toll on American soldiers, 148 of whom were killed in battle. Hundreds of other soldiers returned home with serious injuries. Still others suffered from mysterious physical and emotional problems that lasted long after the war had ended. In addition to the impact on U.S. troops, the Gulf War had negative consequences for American relations in the Middle East.

## Gulf War Syndrome

Following the war, many American soldiers who had fought in the Persian Gulf began to feel sick. Their symptoms were both physical and mental. They included fatigue, joint and muscle pain, loss of mobility, headaches, problems with memory and concentration, and rashes. Doctors saw a similar set of symptoms in tens of thousands of Gulf War veterans, and the sickness became known as Gulf War syndrome. Naming the disorder, however, proved much easier than explaining it.

At first, many doctors dismissed the veterans' symptoms as posttraumatic stress disorder (PTSD). PTSD is often found among people who have experienced severe trauma, and it's fairly common among war veterans. Eventually, most doctors agreed that Gulf War syndrome was different from PTSD. But they couldn't explain what caused the illness. Theories include exposure to chemical or biological weapons, smoke and ash from burning oil wells, and vaccinations and medications used during combat.

## September 11, 2001

There is no direct relationship between the 1991 Persian Gulf War and the September 11 terrorist attacks against America. But there is a significant link. On September 11, 2001, terrorists hijacked four U.S. jetliners headed on cross-country trips. The hijackers crashed two of the planes into the World Trade Center skyscrapers in New York City. A third plane was flown into the Pentagon building outside Washington, D.C. The hijackers of the fourth plane most likely intended to hit another high-profile building in Washington, D.C., but that plane never made it to its destination. Instead, it crashed in a field in Pennsylvania.

The U.S. government has named Osama bin Laden as the prime suspect in these terrorist attacks that killed thousands of people. The hijackers were members of bin Laden's Al Qaeda terrorist network. Bin Laden hates the United States government and all American citizens. This hatred stems in large part from U.S. involvement in Middle Eastern affairs. Bin Laden was particularly enraged by U.S. troops being stationed in Saudi Arabia during and after the Gulf War. To Osama bin Laden, the September 11 terrorist attacks were most likely a form of retaliation for this and other

A supporter of Muttahida Majlis-e-Amal (an alliance of six Islamic parties), holds a poster of Iraqi President Saddam Hussein and Al Qaeda leader Osama bin Laden during an anti-war rally in Quetta, Pakistan, in 2003. The rally protested the U.S.-led invasion of Iraq.

"crimes" he feels that the United States has committed against the Arab world.

## Gulf War of 2003

In 2003—twelve years after the 1991 Gulf War—U.S. and British troops returned to the Persian Gulf. Saddam Hussein was not complying with the terms of the 1991 cease-fire agreement. Iraq had failed to cooperate with UN inspectors sent to check for weapons of mass destruction. By 1998, Iraq had refused to allow the UN weapons inspectors to even enter the country. At the end of 2002, Iraq did allow the inspectors to return. But the U.S. government still believed that Iraq was producing weapons of mass destruction. Despite the lack of UN approval, the United States launched a military campaign against Iraq—called Operation Iraqi Freedom—in March 2003.

### Exile of Saddam Hussein

The U.S. government had two main goals for the 2003 Gulf War. One goal was to make sure that Iraq could not manufacture weapons of mass destruction. The other goal was to remove Saddam Hussein from power. In April 2003, coalition forces seized Iraq's capital city of Baghdad. Saddam Hussein was forced to flee from the area, thereby giving up control of the Iraqi government.

### Withdrawal of U.S. Troops

Following the first Gulf War, about 5,000 U.S. troops remained stationed in Saudi Arabia. The Saudi government

Smoke bellows into the Iraqi sky after a building is hit in central Baghdad after a coalition air raid on Monday, March 31, 2003.

allowed these troops to stay in the country to enforce a no-fly zone over southern Iraq. When the 2003 Gulf War began, the number of U.S. troops in Saudi Arabia doubled from 5,000 to 10,000. On May 1, 2003, President George W. Bush declared the end of major combat operations in Iraq. At that time, the United States also decided to end military operations in Saudi Arabia. The U.S and Saudi governments mutually agreed that the United States would remove most of its troops from the region.

Now that the initial threat from Iraq has waned, the United States has withdrawn most of its forces from Saudi Arabia. Here, U.S. Secretary of Defense Donald Rumsfeld speaks to coalition troops at Prince Sultan Air Base in Al Kharj, Saudi Arabia, in April 2003.

The presence of U.S. troops in Saudi Arabia had angered many people in the Middle East. Saudi Arabia is home to two of the holiest sites of Islam. Many Muslims believe that non-Muslims should not be allowed on this holy land. The withdrawal of U.S. troops from Saudi Arabia may help to ease tensions between the United States and Arab nations.

# GLOSSARY

**alliance**  An association of nations that share common interests or goals.

**altitude**  The height of an object above land.

**ammunition**  Explosive military items, such as bombs.

**amphibious**  Relating to both land and water.

**antiaircraft**  Designed for defense against air attack.

**atrocity**  An act of an extremely cruel or brutal nature.

**casualty**  A person who was killed, usually during a war or conflict.

**cease-fire**  A military order to end fighting.

**civilian**  A person who is not on active military duty.

**coalition**  A temporary alliance of nations formed for a joint purpose.

**dictator**  A leader who rules absolutely.

**deployment**  The act of placing military troops in combat position.

**embargo**  A prohibition on commerce.

**fundamentalist**  A person who follows a movement that emphasizes strict obedience to a set of principles or beliefs.

**hostage**  A person taken by force in order to obtain the taker's demands.

**humanitarian**  Promoting human welfare.

**import**  To bring merchandise into one country from another country.

**Islam**  The religious faith of Muslims.

**Kurds**  Members of a group of people who live in connecting areas of certain Middle Eastern countries, including Iraq, Iran, Turkey, and Syria.

**Muslim**  A follower of the religion of Islam.

**rebellion**  A resistance or opposition to an established government.

**refugee**  A person who flees from a country to escape danger.

**resolution**  A formal expression of intent voted by an official organization.

**sanction**  A military or economic measure used to force a nation to comply with international law.

**slant drilling**  A type of oil drilling in which the drill is forced into a slanted direction, rather than its usual vertical direction.

**sortie**  A mission or attack by one plane.

**surrender**  To give up.

**veteran**  A person who formerly served in the armed forces.

# FOR MORE INFORMATION

## Organizations

Amnesty International USA
322 Eighth Avenue
New York, NY 10001
Web site: http://www.amnestyusa.org

Anti-Defamation League (ADL)
823 United Nations Plaza
New York, NY 10017
Web site: http://www.adl.org

Council on American-Islamic Relations
453 New Jersey Avenue SE
Washington, DC 20003
Web site: http://www.cair-net.org

National Council on U.S.-Arab Relations
1140 Connecticut Avenue NW, Suite 1210
Washington, DC 20036
Web site: http://www.ncusar.org

## Web Sites

Due to the changing nature of Internet links, the Rosen
Publishing Group, Inc., has developed an online list of Web
sites related to the subjects of this book. This site is updated
regularly. Please use this link to access the list:

http://www.rosenlinks.com/wcme/guwa

# FOR FURTHER READING

Cipkowski, Peter. *Understanding the Crisis in the Persian Gulf*. New York: John Wiley & Sons, 1992.

Deegan, Paul J. *Operation Desert Storm*. Edina, MN: Abdo & Daughters, 1991.

Foster, Leila Merrell. *The Story of the Persian Gulf War* (Cornerstones of Freedom). Chicago: Children's Book Press, 1991.

Gay, Kathlyn, and Martin Gay. *Persian Gulf War* (Voices from the Past). New York: Twenty-First Century Books, 1997.

Holden, Henry M. *The Persian Gulf War* (U.S. Wars). Berkeley Heights, NJ: Enslow Publishers, Inc., 2003.

Kent, Zachary. *The Persian Gulf War: "The Mother of All Battles"* (American War). Hillside, NJ: Enslow Publishers, Inc., 1994.

Steins, Richard. *The Mideast After the Gulf War* (Headliners). Brookfield, CT: Millbrook Press, 1992.

# BIBLIOGRAPHY

Cormier, William R. "Special Report: War in the Persian Gulf." World Book Online. Retrieved May 27, 2003 (http://www.worldbookonline.com).

Deegan, Paul J. *Operation Desert Storm*. Edina, MN: Abdo & Daughters, 1991.

Deese, David A. "Persian Gulf War of 1991." World Book Online. Retrieved May 21, 2003 (http://www.worldbookonline.com).

Encyclopaedia Britannica. "Persian Gulf War." Retrieved May 21, 2003 (http://www.britannica.com).

Gay, Kathlyn, and Martin Gay. *Persian Gulf War* (Voices from the Past). New York: Twenty-First Century Books, 1997.

Holden, Henry M. *The Persian Gulf War* (U.S. Wars). Berkeley Heights, NJ: Enslow Publishers, Inc., 2003.

King, John. *The Gulf War*. New York: Dillon Press, 1991.

Steins, Richard. *The Mideast After the Gulf War* (Headliners). Brookfield, CT: Millbrook Press, 1992.

# INDEX

## A
air assault, 4, 7, 25–27, 29, 31, 33, 40
Aziz, Tariq, 40

## B
Baath Party, 14
Baghdad, 4, 14, 25, 54
Baker, James, 40
bin Laden, Osama, 52–54
Bush, George H. W., 6–7, 19, 20–21, 29, 30, 35, 39, 40
Bush, George W., 56

## E
Egypt, 14, 21, 29, 37

## F
Faud, King, 18
France, 21, 39

## G
Gorbachev, Mikhail, 33
Great Britain, 13, 21, 37, 54
ground assault, 33, 35, 37–39, 40
Gulf War
    coalition casualties in, 22, 43, 51
    coalition of troops in, 4, 7, 20–21, 29, 31
    end of, 7, 39–41
    events leading up to, 5–7, 18
    legacy of, 43
    preparations for, 18–21
    start of, 4, 7, 9, 25, 40
    timeline of, 40
    U.S. aftermath of, 51–54
    weapons used by U.S. in, 26
    women in, 22
Gulf War syndrome, 51–52

## H
Hussein, Saddam
    after Gulf War, 43, 48, 49
    and Gulf War, 27–29, 35, 37, 43
    invading Iran, 9
    and invasion of Kuwait, 5, 6, 7, 9, 11–13, 15, 17, 18, 40
    life of, 4
    removed from power, 14, 41, 54

## I
Iran, 5, 9, 11, 13, 31, 49, 50
Iran-Iraq War, 5, 9–11
Iraq
    after war, 47–51
    casualties from war, 33, 47, 48
    economy of, 5, 11, 13, 17–18, 47–48, 49
    and end of war, 39–41
    invasion of Kuwait, 5–7, 9, 11–15, 17, 18, 44
    location of, 4
    preparing for war, 21–23
    response to air assault, 27–31
    2003 invasion of, 14, 54–56
    UN sanctions against, 17–18, 40, 41, 47–48, 49
Israel, 6, 27–29, 35

## K
Khomeini, Ayatollah, 11
Kurds, 49–51
Kuwait
after Gulf War, 43–44
    atrocities in, 18
    disputes with Iraq, 11–15
    and Gulf War, 23, 25, 33–39, 40, 41, 43
    invasion of by Iraq, 5–7, 9, 15, 17, 18
    and oil, 11–15, 17, 43, 44–47
    rebuilding, 46–47

## O
oil, 5, 9, 11–15, 17, 43, 44–47
Operation Desert Shield, 7, 21

Operation Desert Storm, 7, 25, 26
Organization of Petroleum Exporting
        Countries (OPEC), 11–13

**P**
Persian Gulf, 5, 9, 13, 21, 35, 37, 44
Powell, Colin, 21, 30

**R**
Reagan, Ronald, 19, 30
Republican Guard, 27, 37
Rumaila oil field, 13–15

**S**
Saudi Arabia, 6, 7, 15, 21, 23, 27,
        29, 37–39

and oil, 17
and U.S. troops, 18–20, 52, 54–57
Schwarzkopf, H. Norman, 21, 35,
        36, 37
September 11, 2001, terrorist attacks,
        52–54
Shiite Muslims, 49, 50–51
Syria, 14, 21, 29, 37

**U**
United Nations (UN)/United Nations
        Security Council, 6, 9, 15, 35,
        39, 54
deadline for Iraq, 7, 23, 25, 40
sanctions on Iraq, 17–18, 40, 41,
        47–49

## About the Author

Suzanne J. Murdico is a freelance writer who has authored numerous books for children and teens. She lives near Tampa, Florida, with her husband Vinnie, and their cat Zuzu.

### Photo Credits

Cover, pp. 36, 38, 50 © Peter Turnley/Corbis; pp. 1, 6, 30, 42–43, 48 © Corbis; p. 3 © John McCutcheon/AP/World Wide Photos; pp. 4–5 © Dominique Molland/AP/World Wide Photos; pp. 8–9, 45 © AP/World Wide Photos; pp. 10, 24–25 © Francoise de Mulder/Corbis; p. 12 © Heini Schneebeli/Corbis; pp. 14, 16–17, 53 © Reuters New Media Inc./Corbis; p. 19 © Wally McNamee/Corbis; pp. 20, 34 © Jacques Langevin/Corbis; p. 22 © Bill Gentile/Corbis; p. 28 © David H. Wells/Corbis; pp. 32–33 © Patrick Durand/Corbis; p. 46 © Robert van der Hilst/AP/Corbis; p. 55 © Jerome Delay/AP/World Wide Photos; p. 56 © Luke Frazza/AP/World Wide Photos.

**Designer:** Nelson Sá; **Editor:** Mark Beyer;
**Photo Researcher:** Nelson Sá.

DISCARDED

J 956.70442 MURDICO
Murdico, Suzanne J.
The Gulf War /

PEACHTREE

JUN 15 2004

Atlanta-Fulton Public Library